Career Discovery

Careers If You Like Music

Laura Roberts

ReferencePoint Press®

San Diego, CA

© 2018 ReferencePoint Press, Inc.
Printed in the United States

For more information, contact:
ReferencePoint Press, Inc.
PO Box 27779
San Diego, CA 92198
www.ReferencePointPress.com

LIBRARY OF CONGRESS CATALOGING-IN-PUBLICATION DATA

Name: Roberts, Laura
Title: Careers If You Like Music/by Laura Roberts.
Description: San Diego, CA: ReferencePoint Press, 2018. | Series: Career Discovery | Includes
    bibliographical references and index. |
Identifiers: LCCN 2017014678 (print) | LCCN 2017014943 (ebook) | ISBN 9781682821398 (eBook)
    | ISBN 9781682821381 (hardback)
Subjects: LCSH: Music—Vocational guidance—Juvenile literature.
Classification: LCC ML3795 (ebook) | LCC ML3795 .R597 2018 (print) | DDC 780.23--dc23
LC record available at https://lccn.loc.gov/2017014678

CONTENTS

Introduction: Musicians Are Everywhere

Musicians are everywhere. When most people think of what it's like to work as a musician, they probably picture artists who put songs on the radio, videos on YouTube, or perform live in concert. But guess what? There are a lot of jobs that focus on music that don't involve being a rock star or even a performer. Since music is everywhere, it stands to reason that musicians are everywhere too.

Think about your favorite television shows. Musicians created the theme songs that play in the opening credits of all those shows. They also wrote the scores—and even the background noises and sound effects—for your favorite movies and video games. If you have ever heard a jingle in a commercial that got stuck in your head, it's because musicians were hard at work to craft that catchy tune.

Many Paths to Pro

Students who want to work in the music industry can take many different career paths there. Some will create their own music, and others will help musicians market their work to audiences. Some may teach the next generation of musicians; some may show people how music can provide comfort and healing in therapeutic settings. Still others may create apps for cell phones that can help both amateur and professional musicians record and create music digitally or share their music with fans. Not everyone who works in the music business, of course, needs to play music. But those who are interested in performance have plenty of options, and those who enjoy being in the background can also find challenging, fun work in the field, whether working as assistants to musicians, record producers, or technicians in a studio setting.

A Mentally and Physically Demanding Career

Musical careers require both mental and physical stamina. Performers need to spend a lot of time focusing themselves inward to be able to write songs and to practice their instruments or singing. Musicians must practice every day to keep their instruments and voices in top form. They must also take care of their bodies, which often double as their instruments. For example, the singer Céline Dion is famous for only whispering on her days off to ensure that her impressive vocal cords will function best when she needs to perform. These kinds of actions may seem extreme to those not in the music industry, but they are common methods of self-care that musicians adopt to perform their best.

Passion versus Payment

An important thing to remember about careers in music is that many are often more about passion than payment. This is not to say that musicians can't (or don't) get paid; however, nearly all musicians and music lovers who work in jobs that center directly on musical performance talk about their passion for performing more than the size of the paychecks they receive. Musical careers are about harnessing a freedom to create, indulging in play, sharing emotions and songs with others, and connecting with other people through song. No matter what genre or style, everyone who truly loves music and wants to make it for a living seeks time and space to create and to connect organically with their audience.

The Bureau of Labor Statistics notes that music is often a secondary career for many musicians, who either need or want a day job to support their musical activities. However, there are many different ways musicians can build legitimate, full-time careers. Choreographers, dancers, operatic performers, and symphony orchestra members all earn a living by performing in a wide variety of roles. Some musicians may take their music straight to live audiences, performing at local clubs. Others may play in offbeat spaces—perhaps even performing in parks or public transit stations—to earn money. Still others may aim to sign with a record label to get help marketing and distributing their songs. Some may perform only on recorded music, either as principal or backup musicians. Teachers and music therapists teach others how to play instruments or sing. There is, ultimately, no one *right* way to make it in the music business.

Musician

What Do Musicians Do?

Musicians play music, of course. But pop stars and rock bands are just the tip of the iceberg when it comes to having a career in music. Musicians may play as part of a band or orchestra or perform as soloists. They may write and release their own music or create and record music for other artists. They might be studio musicians who record jingles for commercials. They may create the songs and sound effects used in film and television soundtracks, video games, apps, and software. They may be live performers who are part of a symphony orchestra or smaller ensemble groups, or they may perform in operas or other theatrical productions, like musicals. Some may be background vocalists who work live events or record in the studio, supporting celebrities. Others work for religious organizations leading choirs or performing as a cantor, which is a singer in a Jewish synagogue. Still others perform at different cultural or celebratory events like weddings or bar and bat mitzvahs.

Musicians usually specialize in a specific genre of music. Some stick to rock and pop, writing the catchy songs that get stuck in your head. Others are classically trained, working from sheet music with symphony orchestras to re-create music from bygone eras. Jazz and blues musicians improvise new riffs on old standards or create new sonic landscapes while stretching the limits of their instruments' capabilities. Hip-hop artists engage in rap battles and create potent political commentary with their spoken-word lyrics, music samples, and unique beats.

A Typical Day on the Job

As with most performing artists, there is no typical day in the life of a musician. All musicians split their time between practicing, performing, and writing music. They must also take care of the administrative tasks related to their career, such as returning e-mails, paying bills, and making sure they have gigs lined up. That said, there are important differences between the daily life of traveling musicians and those who work in studios.

Traveling musicians are often responsible for making their own touring arrangements. This means they need to book their own airfare and car rentals. They also need to line up hotel rooms or other accommodations. "It's no secret that in today's industry, musicians are much more than musicians," says guitarist Lee Duck. "During the early stages of touring with my band Sky Eats Airplane, I often served as a de facto tour manager and booking agent."[1]

Independent performers are also frequently in charge of selling their own merchandise at shows. Meeting and greeting fans (and signing autographs) is therefore a regular part of the routine. In addition, unless they've got a dedicated crew of roadies to help out, they are also responsible for bringing in their gear before a show and packing things up at the end of the night. As musician Alex White of the band White Mystery explains,

> We'll arrive at the venue, and sometimes that's our first meal of the day at 7:00 p.m., because we're fueled by coffee and snacks. We set up our merch [merchandise] when we walk in the door, then basically play pinball until the doors open at 9:00 p.m., and man the merch table until the show, which is usually around 11:00 p.m. or midnight. And then we play, then we party until three in the morning.[2]

Studio musicians, on the other hand, typically spend more time in one location. They can often be found practicing and working in the studio, where they write or revise songs and lay down tracks (record). Or they may simply be required to show up at the studio on time to perform their parts.

How Do You Become a Musician?

There are many different ways to become a professional musician. Some people audition for a role in a band or orchestral group. Others may record their own music in a home or rented studio space. Whether musicians work as soloists or as part of a band, many choose to take their music directly to their audiences via the

Be an Artist

"There are many musicians, but few real artists. True artists remake and replenish themselves perpetually, and are the ones followed by a loyal public. Decide what you need in order to honestly call yourself an artist and go get it. Study the people you consider to be great artists and emulate them. You can't go wrong by spending a day as Mendelssohn, Picasso or Charlie Chaplin. Put yourselves in their heads and you'll see the world differently."

—David Finckel, cellist

David Finckel "10 Habits of Successful Musicians," *Strad*, February 11, 2014. www.thestrad.com.

Internet. YouTube, SoundCloud, and other music apps have made selling individual songs or full albums straight to fans a viable alternative to signing a mainstream record deal. Still other musicians are hired by a record label or by a headline artist to perform on tour.

Some musicians may be hired purely on a gig basis, meaning that they only play one show at a given venue. Others may be hired on longer contracts, which include a series of performance dates. This is usually the case with a touring group or a Las Vegas–style show where the artists are in residence at a certain venue for a set period of time (usually between six months and one year, though shows that sell well can hold residencies for several years).

Ultimately, there are many ways to become a musician. Indeed, as musician Tom Hess puts it, the secret to becoming a professional musician is to get your mind into the right space to tackle many challenges, and be sure you have the "total package." As he explains on his blog,

> In addition to doing all the stuff that music students do (taking guitar lessons, reading about music, listening to music, practicing my instrument, jamming with friends, forming bands and dreaming about making it), I figured I needed to do more than the obvious (improving as a musician). I needed to try to discover how to become a professional guitarist, how to create luck, how to know where

the right place and right time is (and then figure out how to get there), how to get discovered, how to become more talented faster, and how to make key contacts with people in the music industry.[3]

It is important for all musicians to figure out what they want to do with their musical career (become a solo or ensemble musician, play with studio musicians on recordings or give live performances, and so on) so they can figure out how to take their work from the hobby level to the pro level.

Do You Need a College Degree?

Some musicians need an advanced music degree for the type of career they want to pursue, but others argue that there is no point in going deep into debt for a diploma. *Paste Magazine* conducted an informal survey of twenty working musicians, asking them about their college diplomas. The magazine discovered that most respondents credited their alma maters with developing their critical-thinking and writing skills, and some walked away with technical skills that help them in the music industry. However, those with liberal arts majors tended not to use their degrees directly in their work.

That said, some kinds of music degrees can be helpful, particularly for musicians looking for industry contacts or highly specialized skills. Opera singers, for instance, tend to require more advanced degrees than pop stars. Music performance degrees can help musicians and vocalists hone their technique. Therefore, a bachelor's degree in music or music performance is recommended for those interested in learning the basics of most performance genres, and a master's degree or doctorate may be necessary for musicians in the classical sphere.

Practice makes perfect, particularly when it comes to musicianship. No matter what style of music they play, all musicians need several hours of practice each day to keep their skills sharp. When first starting out, musicians will likely need to take lessons from a private instructor. Once they have progressed, however, more seasoned musicians typically prefer to practice on their own and will then practice with their groups to perfect their performance. A conductor or music director will lead larger groups, like symphony orchestras; in a rock band, the lead singer is often in charge of rehearsals.

Personality and Skills

Musicians need to be able to face rejection with a smile, as at least half of the job involves putting yourself out in front of an audience and performing. Both talent and persistence are important traits for musicians since rejection may continue for years. Musicians must also be hardworking and have the ability to keep practicing, writing new material, and networking to land new gigs and build good relationships with potential clients and bandmates.

Earning a Living

The Bureau of Labor Statistics says that the average annual salary of a musician is $50,336. The field is expected to grow at a rate of 3 percent through 2024. Although this is considered slow by some industry standards, it is still positive news for those who are passionate about earning a living in the field of music. Additionally, the type of music that is performed can significantly influence a musician's salary. The Berklee College of Music explains that there is a wide range in pay scales for musicians of different types, from $50 to $100 a day for street performers to $1,000 to $2,500 per gig for cover bands. Casino performers in a Las Vegas residency can earn $500,000, and an arena-level headliner can earn up to $30 million for a forty-date tour. With such a huge range of earning potential, it is important for musicians to be clear on their goals both for performance and payment.

Musicians say one of their biggest challenges is that they often wear too many hats. This is particularly true of independent artists, who are tasked with running all aspects of their careers;

Dream Big, but Be Realistic

"Depending on the path you take in the wide world of music, it's possible that you may never have a stable income. Even if it is stable, it might take years or even decades before it's large enough for you to have certain luxuries. This doesn't have to be a source of fear or anxiety as long as you know how to live within your means. Try to create some kind of stable cash flow in order to cover certain expenses such as gas, food or utilities. . . . That way, you can take a few things off your mind while doing your budgeting and focus more on making rent."

—Dylan Welsh, a freelance musician and music journalist

Dylan Welsh, "6 Qualities That All Successful Musicians Have," *Sonicbids Blog*, June 30, 2014. http://blog.sonicbids.com.

they create and record music, mix and edit it, promote their own shows, and keep track of finances. These day-to-day activities may threaten to overwhelm a musician who just wants to play an instrument or sing. Indie artists must figure out how to balance performing and recording with the myriad assorted tasks they must complete in order to keep their careers moving forward. Alternately, delegating some of this work to a personal assistant or outsourcing more of the busy work can prove useful.

Find Out More

American Federation of Musicians of the United States and Canada
www.afm.org

This is the largest union of musicians in the world, offering musicians the opportunity to organize so they can, as a group, demand higher salaries and better treatment from employers. The organization also offers musicians useful information about how to travel with their instruments to avoid incurring damage on commercial flights.

American Guild of Musical Artists

www.musicalartists.org

This is a labor union that represents artists from numerous disciplines that create America's operatic, dance, and choral heritage.

American Guild of Organists

www.agohq.org

The American Guild of Organists website is devoted to helping organists study their instrument and find jobs.

Music Conductor and Director

What Does a Conductor Do?

Conductors and music directors lead bands, orchestras, choirs, and other musical groups for a living. They work with studio musicians on recordings or lead groups of musicians during live performances, such as a symphony orchestra. In addition to conducting music, they have a variety of behind-the-scenes duties that help keep the group running smoothly. Conductors will typically choose all the pieces that the group performs, and hire permanent members and guest performers. They are also responsible for leading rehearsals and interpreting musical scores. As the group's most public member, conductors also represent musicians at fund-raising events, where they need to make good connections with donors.

In contrast, music directors typically lead musical groups that perform under the banner of a school or church organization. They may be responsible for leading middle school, high school, or college groups; community youth groups; or church groups. Some music directors are even in charge of orchestras that perform with other artistic

Accept That You Are a "Waiter"

"The composer is the chef and conductors are the waiters. Both are totally honourable professions but we have to accept that if I conduct a piece by Beethoven, I'm just a waiter. I might be head waiter, but waiter none the less and I am there to make sure the food comes to the table on time and intact."

—Esa-Pekka Salonen, conductor of the Philharmonia Orchestra in London

Quoted in Alison Feeney-Hart, "Esa-Pekka Salonen: 10 Tips to Becoming a Conductor," BBC News, November 30, 2013. www.bbc.com.

companies, such as dance or opera troupes. Like conductors, music directors help musicians rehearse. They help musicians keep time and help the group achieve balance between different sections. Choirs are typically divided into soprano, alto, tenor, and baritone sections, and the music director helps make sure each section is heard (or that different sections stand out at certain times).

A Typical Day on the Job

A typical day for an orchestra conductor includes both an intense round of conducting and a good deal of alone time; this is so the conductor can think about the way he or she wants the group to perform each piece. Consider how Tara Simoncic, the associate conductor for the Greenwich Symphony in Greenwich, Connecticut, spends her day. "When I'm not in rehearsal or performance, I spend a great deal of time studying and developing my own interpretation of the music," she told the *Guardian* newspaper. "If I'm conducting a ballet, I study the choreography as well as the music. . . . On the podium, I am either rehearsing for around three hours at a time or performing. When rehearsing, I pick things apart and try to get exactly the sound and interpretation from the orchestra that I have in mind."[4] Simoncic notes that rehearsal time is sometimes strictly limited, particularly when directing an orchestra that is performing with a ballet troupe, for example. She must therefore be extremely well prepared when she picks up her baton so as not to waste the performers' time.

In addition to conducting music—which is the most fun part of the job—conductors are often responsible for representing their orchestra to the public. Joseph Young, the assistant conductor for the Atlanta Symphony Orchestra, notes this in an interview published on CareersInMusic.com. "You are looked at as the professional face," he says. "It's a very public job where you are in the public [eye] a lot. It can be a very social, community-related job where you are a community figure and looked up to."[5] Indeed, conductors are often asked to socialize with potential donors, patrons of the arts, and other benefactors who might make charitable contributions to their organizations. They must make sure they are both polite and charming enough to get potential donors to become actual donors.

Do You Need a College Degree?

Aspiring conductors typically require a master's degree in music theory, music composition, or conducting. Choir directors may only require a bachelor's degree. Music programs generally teach students about music history and musical styles, in addition to the basics of composing and conducting. When applying to a music degree program, applicants must either audition in person or submit recordings of their performances—or sometimes both. This process is similar to submitting a portfolio for admission to an arts program.

Musical directors and conductors are typically classically trained at a very young age and often on multiple instruments. Private lessons, as well as membership in a school band, orchestra, or choir are encouraged, as is additional training that can be obtained via fellowships or music camps. Any classes, lessons, or opportunities to perform with a group are ideal for budding conductors in order to both learn to play music and to observe other conductors' styles.

Personality and Skills

Conductors and music directors usually have strong personalities. They are often colorful characters with larger-than-life presences onstage. Although they must be musically literate, it is just as important for conductors to have good interpersonal skills. Being able to work with a wide variety of people, including musicians, agents, recording engineers, and other behind-the-scenes staff is critical to a conductor's success. They must also be friendly and have respect for all of the people involved in the group. Whereas conductors of the past had a reputation for being curmudgeonly (perhaps because they also frequently composed the works being performed), today's conductors must genuinely enjoy working with other people and spend a lot of time with them in both professional and social settings. Since conductors are also responsible for interacting with donors, it is important for them to have great social skills.

In addition to interpersonal skills, conductors must also be great leaders. A conductor must frequently lead by example, by being the first to arrive at a performance or rehearsal space and the last to leave. Conductors are also involved in the arrangement of musical pieces and must rewrite them to highlight different sections of the band or orchestra, depending on the group's size and desired sound. They must also help their musicians deliver their very best performances. Sometimes this requires singing or playing a bit of the piece in question, especially technically challenging passages, to illustrate the kind of sound they want their musicians to achieve. This, of course, means that conductors must also have musical talent.

Finally, most successful conductors possess perseverance and discipline. Although talent is certainly a key ingredient to succeeding at the job, consistent practice is also necessary. It may take many years for conductors to find the best fit for their conducting style, and they may move from one city to another in search of their ideal orchestra. Sometimes conductors may find themselves out of work due to budgetary constraints or cuts.

Music Directors in Action

"At Trinity [Church] there's an 8 o'clock, a 9 o'clock, a 10 o'clock and an 11:15 service. And I usually am the person that's doing the music at the 11:15 service, but I have to be a presence at the 9 and 10, because the 9 o'clock has the youth group. It's a new program and we're excited about it. And on the Sundays when Trinity Choir is singing, I'll do a rehearsal at 10 a.m., and then the service will start at 11:15. I will either conduct that or play and conduct or just play. That service usually finishes at 1. . . . My Sunday afternoons have been quite sporadic. But the thing that we like to do is go home and cook, and then I'll study scores as well."

—Julian Wachner, music director for Trinity Wall Street Church

John Leland, "A Day of Music, and Movement Therapy, for a Conductor," *New York Times*, December 22, 2013. www.nytimes.com.

Being able to remain upbeat and keep working in an uncertain industry is therefore another critical ingredient for a conductor.

Working Conditions

Music directors and conductors typically work in concert halls and recording studios, directing music. They may also work in schools, churches, synagogues, or temples. Travel is frequently required, whether locally or further afield to different performance spaces. Music directors and conductors can be found all across the United States, but more jobs (along with better pay and higher status) are typically located in big cities with entertainment districts. Chicago, Los Angeles, Nashville, San Fransisco, and New York are considered some of the top cities in the United States for the performing arts, and competition for jobs in these hubs tends to be more fierce than in smaller cities with lesser-known orchestras.

Earning a Living

A conductor's pay can vary widely. The Bureau of Labor Statistics (BLS) reports that conductors have an average annual salary of about $49,820. For choir, orchestra, or opera conductors, the Berklee College of Music cites a range from $15,000 to $275,000 a year. Conductors of major symphonies and opera companies typically earn toward the higher end of that pay scale, working about forty weeks a year. Conductors on the lower end of the scale usually direct smaller organizations and may work fewer weeks per year. A conductor for the Durham Symphony in North Carolina, for instance, receives between $26,000 to $36,000 a year.

Directors of church choirs are typically paid less than symphony conductors, and Berklee cites a range from $5,000 to $70,000 a year. These salaries are based on the number of hours worked each week (ranging from ten to forty), the size of the church's congregation, and the director's level of education.

What Is the Future Outlook for Conductors?

Conductors will always be needed to fill positions in top symphonies around the world as well as to lead school bands and orchestras. Although the BLS suggests that, compared to other occupations, the growth rate for music directors and conductors is relatively slow (just 3 percent through 2024), this should not discourage anyone interested in pursuing this career. This is because the BLS also notes that

> the number of people attending musical performances, such as symphonies and concerts, and theatrical performances, such as ballets and musical theater, is expected to increase moderately. Music directors will be needed to lead orchestras for concerts and musical theater performances. They also will conduct the music that accompanies ballet troupes and opera companies.[6]

For students excited about conducting and directing music, there will always be new and interesting opportunities to direct performance pieces.

Find Out More

Band Director

www.banddirector.com

This online hub for band directors, including high school and college directors and marching band directors, features a variety of information on conducting, fund-raising, and running band camps.

College Orchestra Directors Association

http://codaweb.org

This association is aimed at working orchestra directors at the college level. It offers a variety of initiatives, news and resources, and information on promotion and tenure, touring, ideas for programs, and scholarly material.

Conductors' Guild Inc.

www.conductorsguild.org

A group dedicated to helping conductors find jobs and opportunities to study the art of conducting.

League of American Orchestras

www.americanorchestras.org

This group aims to support American orchestras and orchestral performers, including music directors and conductors. It also publishes *Symphony* magazine, a quarterly magazine that reports on issues, trends, personalities, and news in the orchestral world.

Music Journalist

What Does a Music Journalist Do?

Music journalists are journalists who write about the music industry. Many people have a glamorous view of this job, picturing interviews with their favorite musicians while attending parties with rock stars. However, this is still a job that requires discipline, like any other.

Music journalists write reviews of albums and concerts. They also profile musicians and bands, report on music news, and interview musicians. Music journalists research their subjects by watching them perform and listening to their music. They then write up reviews or profile pieces. It is very common for music journalists to work within their favorite genre of music since the work is so all-consuming. Ultimately, most music journalists say they are passionate about what they do, and their work requires them to live and breathe the music they love.

To write good reviews, music journalists must be fair, balanced, and honest. They need to say what they *really* think of the latest album, even if it goes against popular opinion. Music journalist Lina Lecaro points out that all music journalists must put their careers before any rock star crushes. "A crappy album is still just that," she says. "Critics simply can't not call it like we see it."[7]

Music journalists don't just describe the music they listen to; they also compare and contrast it with a band's previous albums. They also consider where a band fits into their specific genre's musical history. They might ask how the band compares to the great rock bands of the past or how it pushes a particular music genre forward. Music journalists thus have to do their homework in order to make accurate comparisons and assessments.

A Typical Day on the Job

Music journalists typically spend a lot of time at a computer, typing up stories and doing online research. They might listen to music, watch videos, or type madly to meet a deadline. They also need to read other articles by fellow journalists to familiarize themselves with a new band or musician before an interview. They often spend a lot of time e-mailing editors to pitch new ideas for articles or contacting agents, publicists, musicians, and anyone else in the business who may make a good contact for a story.

In addition to using their computers, music journalists can frequently be found on the phone, chasing down leads and recording phone interviews. Music journalists who review concerts start their days later than other kinds of journalists, as they often do their work in local clubs and music venues, which operate at night. They may also attend record releases or after parties to catch musicians in a more relaxed setting, which can sometimes result in more unguarded answers than a formal one-on-one interview.

Do You Need a College Degree?

Music journalists don't necessarily need a college degree to succeed. More important is a love of music and a passion for talking to the people who create it as well as the tenacity to chase down a story. As journalist Jenna Goudreau notes, journalism is a "doing field," and journalists need to get out into the world to find their own stories, sources, and work. She says the best music journalists have "independence, drive and attention to detail, which can't be taught in a classroom."[8]

For those who do get a college degree, majoring in journalism is an obvious choice. Journalism school teaches students how to write stories, find and protect sources, and offers a chance to work on a student publication to learn valuable on-the-job skills. Some examples of schools with reputable journalism programs include Emerson College in Boston; Northwestern University in Evanston, Illinois; and the University of Texas at Austin. Students interested in music journalism can make that the focus of their studies.

What It Takes to Be a Music Journalist

Aside from being a talented writer, a music journalist needs to be a great verbal communicator. Since much of the work involves interviewing people and chasing down contacts for a new story, music journalists must be persuasive and friendly. They must be able to generate good interview questions, sometimes on the fly, and express themselves clearly. Of course, they must always be able to tell their readers a great story that will keep them reading — and coming back for more.

Music journalists should also be creative and think imaginatively. Writers must be able to paint a vivid picture of what a song sounds like for a readership that may not have heard the song before. Being able to compare new songs to older songs by the same musicians, or to the genre of music as a whole, is part of a music journalist's talent. It is also important to be able to synthesize new information and sort through a mental catalog of songs that sound similar to one another, explain why these songs sound similar, and whether this is a good or bad thing for the artist. A good music journalist can explain something complex in language that the average reader finds easy to understand.

It pays for music journalists to have persistence, too. This is because journalists more often hear the word *no* than the word *yes*, and they must sometimes come up with creative ways to turn a rejection into acceptance. Being aggressive, in a polite way, is often the key to a journalist's success. Simply refusing to back down or take no for an answer can often result in a hesitant source agreeing to be interviewed.

Another trait that all music journalists share is their ability to make many different types of people feel comfortable. Journalists must be pushy to get a story, but they also need to know when to back off and let a subject speak. They need to be open-minded enough to interview people from various cultures, socioeconomic backgrounds, races, and religions and not take anything for granted or make any assumptions. They often need to ask difficult questions in ways that do not offend their interviewees.

Music journalist Lisa Robinson notes it is very important to have genuine interactions with celebrities. A good strategy for doing this is to have a good icebreaker ready to open up the conversation. "My best icebreaker was when I met Mick Jagger for the first time," she told *Teen Vogue*. "It was completely natural! I just looked at him and said, 'Those are the tackiest shoes I've ever seen in my life.'

Write What You Want to Write, but Do the Work

"Make sure that you're really focused on [your career] and don't get discouraged. Don't do this if you're trying to get rich. There are some people who make a healthy living, but the reward is being able to say 'I get up in the morning and write about what I wanna write about.' The number one mistake people make when trying to get into this career is not understanding the work that goes into a good story: fact checking, a thesis statement, opening paragraph, closing paragraph. They don't do the work."

—Alvin Blanco, deputy editor of the website Hip-Hop Wired

Quoted in CareersInMusic.com, "Music Journalist." www.careersinmusic.com.

He was wearing these rhinestone-studded shoes, and nobody talked to him that way!"[9] The ability to quickly gain a person's trust or make a subject laugh is critical for a music journalist's success.

Working Conditions

Music journalists are often assumed to work in extremely glamorous conditions because they regularly hobnob with celebrities. However, like any job, there are also downsides. Freelancers may work in a home office or coffee shop, grinding out stories for tight deadlines. They may be required to file a concert review immediately after attending a show, so they may have to work anywhere they can get an Internet connection—or even from their phone. Conducting interviews can also be tricky, as travel schedules can make it difficult or impossible to reach musicians on tour. Journalists may have to travel to a recording studio or music venue to meet up with a band before or after its show, and these environments can be chaotic and stressful. Ultimately, however, music journalists are exactly the kind of people who thrive under these conditions and, therefore, are rarely bored while in pursuit of a story.

Earning a Living

The Bureau of Labor Statistics (BLS) reports that the average journalist's median pay is $37,720 per year, and O*NET (the Occupational Information Network) lists a median salary of $36,360. The job board Payscale.com lists a median salary of $39,381 for journalists and $39,230 for music journalists in particular. The Berklee College of Music reports an average salary between $15,000 and $30,000 for music journalists, with a breakdown of $50 to $150 per review and $100 to $500 for a feature story.

What Is the Future Outlook for Music Journalists?

The BLS predicts that journalism jobs will decline by 9 percent through 2024. However, as digital media becomes a more regular

Build Trust, Not Friendships

"Celebrities are not your friends. You're both using each other: You're using the subject to get a story, and the subject is using you to be in a story. That doesn't mean you can't be friendly with them and develop a certain sort of trust. If you tell someone you're interviewing that something's off the record, keep it off the record! However, I don't think journalists should ever throw themselves into thinking that these people are going to show up at their funeral. . . . I was always in it for the music, not the party."

—Lisa Robinson, music journalist

Quoted in Dana Mathews, "Tips for the Aspiring Music Journalist, from Industry Legend Lisa Robinson," *Teen Vogue*, April 23, 2014. www.teenvogue.com.

part of life, journalism is adapting to changes in the industry. Journalists are developing more of a multimedia approach to reporting news and views online. Music journalists will also have to adapt to this changing landscape. They will have to come out from behind the scenes to produce their own videos or podcasts and self-promote their articles.

In addition, tomorrow's music journalists will need to have a more entrepreneurial spirit, as many journalists will need to work for themselves rather than for a major or traditional media outlet. There is a lot of opportunity in the world of self-employment and independent publications. Indeed, some of the best-known music websites currently in operation—such as *Pitchfork* and *Vice*'s Noisey—started as the creations of college kids with an interest in music who wanted to share their reviews online. It will be important for music journalists to put more thought into how to produce their own media rather than hunting down a traditional job. Therefore, mastering the art of networking and the ever-changing landscape of social media will be key skills in the new world of music journalism.

Find Out More

American Society of Journalists and Authors

www.asja.org

This is a professional organization for journalists of all kinds, including music journalists. It offers networking opportunities, payment and market information, assistance with contracts, awards, mentorship, and various member discounts.

Billboard

www.billboard.com

This is the publisher of the *Billboard* Top 100, which charts the best-selling albums in various genres. Staying on top of trends in the industry, including the best-selling albums (both weekly and historically), is key for a music journalist's success. Bookmark this site and refer to it often.

Music Critics Association of North America

www.mcana.org

This educational organization promotes music criticism in the United States through annual meetings, online resources for aspiring critics, a newsletter, and assorted professional discounts for members.

Rolling Stone

www.rollingstone.com

A biweekly music magazine, featuring some of the best music and long-form journalism in the United States. Since one of the keys to becoming a successful music journalist includes studying publications to pitch stories to, as well as reading other journalists' best work, this is a great place to keep up with the industry trends, along with music news and interviews.

Composer

A Few Facts

Number of Jobs
About 82,100 in 2014*

Median Salary
$49,820*

Educational Requirements
None

Personal Qualities
Musical ability, interpersonal and promotional skills, determination to succeed

Work Settings
Indoors in recording studios, concert halls, practice rooms

Future Job Outlook
Growth of 3 percent through 2024

*Note: Includes composers and conductors

What Does a Composer Do?

Composers create original music for musicians and vocalists to perform. Composers write music in a variety of styles; they may focus on a specific genre of music or dabble in many. Some may be singer/songwriters who work with just one instrument, but others (usually called arrangers) may score (write music) for many instruments in a band or orchestra. Some composers are known as orchestrators. They adapt music written for another medium into orchestral arrangements. In doing so, they assign different parts to various instruments to make certain parts of a piece stand out or to create a specific type of sound. Composers can also provide their own arrangements or orchestration. Some composers work in film or television, producing mood music. Some create jingles, which is music written for commercials. Others create music and sound effects for video games, apps, software, or even appliances.

Composers sometimes write music that stems from their own inspiration and moods. Or, they might be commissioned to write specific types of music for orchestras, bands, operas, dance troupes, theatrical productions, or other performing artists. Educational institutions; professional societies and associations; orchestral groups; and television, film, and commercial production companies are among the kinds of entities that commission composers to write works of music.

Composers are generally freelancers who either write for a specific audience or create an audience of their own through hard work and dedication. Some may also work as teachers in public schools or by offering private lessons.

A Typical Day on the Job

A typical day in the life of a composer is never truly typical. Many composers work several jobs to pay the bills. Composer Daniel Ott, for example, works as a music teacher at several different schools and composes early in the morning before heading out to teach. He says this experience is typical of what it takes to be a composer but also meet life's other requirements. "We take jobs, occasionally outside of our preferred fields, to sustain life," he wrote in a 2012 blog post. "Still, somehow I managed in the past 24 months to compose a 30-min. string quartet, a 4-min. septet, and I'm wrapping up work on a 15-min. piano duo."[10]

Composers generally divide their time between experimenting with different sounds (using instruments or synthesizers to create them); thinking about the melodies and harmonies they'd like to use in a specific song; using a computer to compose and arrange music; orchestrating compositions for different groups; transcribing songs from their heads onto paper or into a computer program; and playing with various voices, instruments, tempos, rhythms, tones, and more to create the best sound possible.

How Do You Become a Composer?

As noted in the *Occupational Outlook Handbook* of the Bureau of Labor Statistics (BLS), composers of popular music typically do

A guitarist composes an original piece of music. Composers sometimes write for themselves, but are often also commissioned to write specific types of music for orchestras, bands, dance troupes, and theatrical productions.

not require any specific education or degree. Although a music education may help composers perfect their craft, ultimately the best test of their work is whether clients buy their compositions. The best composers understand both their craft and their market, and they work hard to create art that balances their need for creative outlet and meets commercial interest.

For those interested in a formal musical education, a music degree at the bachelor's or master's level is a good bet. Some of the top schools for music composition and performance are the Juilliard School and the Manhattan School of Music, both in New York; the Berklee College of Music in Boston; the Thornton School of Music at the University of Southern California; the Herb Alpert School of Music at the University of California, Los Angeles; and the Oberlin Conservatory in Ohio. Students in a traditional music program will take private lessons on their instrument of choice, learn music theory and history, and take additional liberal arts courses. Students who choose a more specific major, such as film scoring or commercial music, will learn additional skills,

It's Not the Destination but the Journey

"What I love most about my job is the variety and the wonderful journey music takes me [on]. Composing can be quite a lonely existence, it's hard and you need to spend lots of time alone getting it done. For me, working on many different projects spanning different media means I continually get to meet lots of different people with diverse ideas. It keeps me excited about writing. I'd never want to be one of those guys that feels that they are just 'churning out stuff.' I feel really lucky that I get to compose every day. The day I stop feeling that is the day I stop being a composer."

—Alexander Rudd, composer

Quoted in Cavendish Music, "A Day in the Life of Composer Alexander Rudd," Little Black Book, April 2016. https://lbbonline.com.

such as how to compose for film, television, and video games; orchestration; arranging; film music editing; production and recording; conducting; entrepreneurship and business; and music production and audio recording.

Personality and Skills

Composers have some of the same personality traits as conductors and musicians. For one, composers need musical talent to create interesting and commercially viable works. Although they don't need to master any particular instrument, they do need to be able to play at least one primary instrument—typically piano or guitar. Composers should be able to play well enough to perform their own music; this is particularly helpful when showing fellow musicians how to execute certain passages or achieve a certain sound.

In addition to musical talent, composers should have strong interpersonal skills. They frequently interact with musicians, agents, conductors, recording engineers, and various other people in the music industry, so it is important that they have a friendly, respectful disposition. Genuinely enjoying working with other musicians is also an important part of working as a composer; spending time in the company of musicians to rehearse or workshop a piece should be part of the fun.

Along with interpersonal skills, composers must also have top-notch promotional skills. A huge part of the job is trying to make a name for oneself, which involves a lot of self-promotion. Composers cannot be shy about getting their names and work out there—in front of audiences, both online and in person. They need to talk to directors, conductors, musicians, and anyone else who might be interested in performing and recording their music. This takes both perseverance and a belief that your work is truly worth someone else's time and attention. Self-promotion also involves building a dedicated fan base and landing more work—part of any freelancer's daily life.

Who's Hiring?

Composers are typically self-employed; very few work full-time for a company. Although some may be employed as staff or house composers at a film, video, or television production studio, the majority are freelancers. Some manage to find composer-in-residence positions at educational institutions or work as college professors while composing their own music. Employers of composers include record companies, music publishers, film and television production companies, musical theater or dance productions, and individual musicians themselves.

Given the gig nature of the industry, it can often be difficult for composers to find steady work. Hopping from job to job can be challenging, but those who love the work do not mind it. "If you can make a living from composition, awesome, you're doing what you love and getting paid for it," says composer Heather Fenoughty. "But if not, as a musician there are so many other skills you've developed that can supplement your addiction to making music, and keep you afloat in the meaner times between projects."[11]

Once composers become well known, they do not have to seek out work as often—clients will typically come to them. Assignments or commissions will then provide composers with a steady stream of work, albeit the work usually comes with certain creative parameters. Clients typically have a certain story, setting, and mood in mind for the work they seek, and composers need to work within those frameworks to provide what their client wants.

Earning a Living

Payment for composers can vary widely, depending on the type of music composed. The BLS reports that composers earn a median income of $49,820 per year. According to the Berklee College of Music, arrangers can earn $20,000 to more than $43,000 a year, and copyists (people who make copies of handwritten scores) and orchestrators (people who adapt music written for another medium into orchestral arrangements) receive a rate that is set by the American Federation of Musicians. These fees vary depending on the length of the piece and the type of employer; work is paid either by the line, the page, or the hour. Commercial writing has even more variations on payment. Commercial jingle composers can make anywhere from $100 to more than $8,000 per commercial. Broadway show arrangers can make $30 to $50 per page, with most scores ranging from six hundred to eight hundred pages in length.

Rates and payment scales differ for television and film composition. Television composers can earn anywhere from $1,500 to $7,500 per thirty-minute episode, $2,000 to $15,000 per sixty-minute episode, and $2,000 to more than $55,000 for television movies. Rates similarly vary for film score composers. Those who work on student films can expect to earn up to $10,000, whereas composers for indie feature films might bring in $2,500 to more than $500,000. Composers of music for studio feature films can expect to earn anywhere from $35,000 to more than $2 million. Video game composers may earn anywhere from $300 to $600 per minute of music; some earn $30,000 to more than $75,000 for different types of games.

Some Composers Wear Many Hats

"'The project I'm recording dialogue and sync sound for is a film that will be included in an upcoming show for Slunglow, 'They Only Come At Night: Resurrection.' Slunglow is a contemporary installation art and theatre company specialising in new work, and as a member of the core creative team I'm called upon not only [to] compose the music and put together sound design for the shows, but I will record a lot of the sound, including dialogue, edit it all together and mix it into the final soundscape."

—Heather Fenoughty, composer

Heather Fenoughty, "A Day in the Life of a Composer," *Heather Fenoughty* (blog), March 16, 2009. www.heather-fenoughty.com.

In addition to the initial payment for creating a piece of music, composers also get paid when their music is used for various commercial purposes. Songs can appear in many different places; a song might appear in an episode of a television show, a movie, or a commercial. To legally use the song, production studios pay composers song-licensing fees—that is, money to feature the song in their television show, movie, commercial, or anywhere else. These payments can range from as little as $250 to $750 for an independent film all the way up to $2.5 million for a top-ten hit on *Billboard*'s Hot 100. Composers also earn income from record sales and performances on radio, television, and other media.

What Is the Future Outlook for Composers?

According to the BLS, there is a slow but steady increase in the job market for composers through 2024; the field is expected to grow at a rate of 3 percent. Composers will be needed to create original music for many different art forms and commercial endeavors. Ballet and musical theater attendance is expected to increase, and scores for film, television, and commercials remain in high demand. That said, there is tough competition for open positions and opportunities due to the large number of people who are interested in becoming composers. The work of the best composers should naturally rise to the top, offering the best opportunities to those who write appealing music and work hard.

Find Out More

American Composers Alliance
www.composers.com

This group is dedicated to promoting the works of composers through performances and recordings.

American Composers Forum
www.composersforum.org

This group is dedicated to nurturing composers and their communities by creating new markets and granting, commissioning, and performing their work.

Broadcast Music Inc.
www.bmi.com

This website acts as broker between songwriters and businesses that want to play their music, advocating on behalf of composers and assisting in the process of selling various rights.

Society of Composers Inc.
www.societyofcomposers.org

A professional society dedicated to the promotion, performance, understanding, and dissemination of new and contemporary music.

Audio Engineer

A Few Facts

Number of Jobs
About 117,200 in 2014

Median Salary
$42,550

Educational Requirements
Associate's or bachelor's degree; voluntary certification

Personal Qualities
Communication skills, computer skills, problem-solving skills, manual dexterity

Work Settings
Indoors in recording studios, concert halls, practice rooms; outdoors in large performance venues

Future Job Outlook
Growth of 7 percent through 2024

What Does an Audio Engineer Do?

Audio engineers are responsible for many behind-the-scenes aspects of creating recorded music. They deal specifically with the technical aspects of recording, such as mixing, mastering, and reproducing sound. They also assist producers and musicians. Some work entirely in studios, but others may specialize in engineering live events. Some may stick to the music industry, but others may branch out to the video game, film, or television industries. In addition to recording music, audio engineers also work on spoken-word recordings, such as audiobook tracks and radio ads. They also record sound effects and dialogue for television and film.

Audio engineers work with a master console that has many different dials, switches, buttons, and meters; these help them monitor and adjust different aspects of a recording's sound. The main part of an engineer's job is to read and adjust these inputs to create the desired sound quality and effects. Audio engineers monitor the volume of different instruments and voices, pitch,

37

Unique Tasks for a Unique Job

"[Dialogue editing involves] editing the voice recordings for the 2 shows I'm currently working on—Doc McStuffins or Henry Hugglemonster—as per the director's notes. We get the raw audio in from the studios and I edit the audio, and that becomes the template for the whole episode. (This is known as a radioplay.) This is where the timing of the episode gets tweaked, with lines being added or removed as required. I try to make the story flow as much as possible, overlapping some lines and tightening up pauses to make the interactions between characters more believable and not just actors saying their lines in isolation. Legibility and finding a good rhythm are massively important."

—Tim O'Donovan, audio engineer

Tim O'Donovan, "A Day in the Life of an Audio Engineer," Brown Bag Films, December 4, 2013. www.brownbagfilms.com.

tone, sound quality (musicians staying on beat and in key), mixing (the levels of each instrument and voice in the song as a whole), and various effects.

Audio engineers are also responsible for helping set up the studio before musicians enter. As such, it is their job to properly place microphones, amplifiers, recording equipment, instruments, cords, and other gear to achieve the best sound quality. Audio engineers must also decide how to arrange musicians when they record. Depending on the number of musicians involved, engineers may place each musician in a soundproof booth. Or, musicians may be placed all together in certain areas of a larger room to allow the sounds to naturally overlap. Once musicians arrive at the studio, engineers will tell them where to go and have them play samples of their music to set the levels for each gauge they are using to monitor a musician's gear. This helps avoid distortion, feedback, or imbalances that might detract from the recording's quality.

During the recording process, audio engineers and producers work together to monitor the sounds produced. Engineers will let musicians know whether they need to record another take, and producers will listen for anything that seems to threaten the recording's quality. Audio engineers may also use apprentices called studio technicians. These professionals help move or re-wire equipment, perform on-the-fly maintenance or tech support, and otherwise help out in the studio.

Once the recording sessions are finished, a special kind of audio engineer mixes the tracks to what is called a master track—the final version of the song or album. These engineers are called sound mixers. During the mixing process, engineers balance the sounds of each individual instrument, set equalization (boosting or reducing certain frequencies, including bass and treble), and manipulate the recording in a variety of ways. They can play with the sound, intensity, effects, speed, and tone.

At the end of the day, audio engineers are some of the most important people involved in the recording process, perfecting the recorded sounds to create the single best overall take possible for each song. As the Recording Connection website notes, "Audio engineering is as much art as it is science, because you're always dealing with new variables, from phantom 'hums' in the gear, to a bad recording due to faulty microphones or placement, to the vocalist who can't get it right after 30 takes."[12] Being able to handle various kinds of uncertainties on the job without becoming stressed out is ultimately the key to success.

A Typical Day on the Job

Audio engineers must often perform a variety of different tasks. Tim O'Donovan, an audio engineer for Brown Bag Labs, reports that on any given day, he may find himself recording or editing dialogue, recording scratch dialogue (which are temporary recordings, made to fill in for absent or unavailable voice actors), creating sound effects, mixing dialogue, or composing music. He also checks his e-mail for new pieces of audio delivered from various studio locations since many of the voice actors on the shows for which he works are in different cities.

Other aspects of his job include working long (and sometimes odd) hours in the studio, dealing with a variety of personalities (including demanding clients, micromanaging producers, and diva personalities), and solving problems in the studio. "The offline video editors often come to me looking for sound effects to bring certain scenes in the animatic [a preliminary version of a movie created using storyboard segments and a soundtrack] to life, or to accentuate certain movements or emotions," he says. "Sometimes . . . a particular effect is arrived at by tweaking, pitch shifting, stretching and/or layering various sounds in order to achieve what the episodic director is looking for."[13]

Do You Need a College Degree?

Audio engineers typically need either a bachelor's or an associate's degree in audio engineering to get started. Apprenticeships or internships are also usually part of a degree program; such hands-on experiences help students get a foot in the door for their first job. This is because audio engineering is an experience-based business; the more you can learn about how the equipment in a sound booth works, the better.

In addition to degree programs, internships, and apprenticeships, some budding audio engineers like to attend conferences where they can learn about the latest techniques and equipment.

To this end, the Audio Engineering Society offers a variety of annual conferences as well as information that can help aspiring audio engineers achieve their goals. Audio engineers may also opt to become certified by the Society of Broadcast Engineers. This certificate shows they can provide professional levels of broadcast engineering and that they are up-to-date with their professional development, which hones their skills and increases their employment potential.

Personality and Skills

Audio engineers must have a variety of skills to succeed. The most important of these is possessing good computer and technical skills. Audio engineers use a lot of software programs and equipment, such as Pro Tools, Logic Pro, Reason, Ableton Live, FL Studio, Sonar, and many more. As such, they must be able to work well with many different kinds of technology, learn on the fly, and deal with a variety of issues that crop up in the studio.

Similarly, audio engineers need good problem-solving skills. Being able to figure out what is causing a problem and fix it is one of the biggest challenges of the job. There are many different pieces of equipment involved; both hardware and software can fail. Being able to quickly deduce the nature of the problem and come up with a good solution is therefore critical. Audio engineers should also be able to stay cool under pressure because most of the job involves solving problems and correcting mistakes.

Finally, audio engineers should be excellent communicators. Sometimes the solution to a problem is simple, such as telling a musician to move a microphone one way or another. Other times audio engineers will need to be able to communicate with the musicians in the studio to determine the problem and how to fix it. Good communication skills also help audio engineers work in teams, which they must do often. Because they typically work in tandem with other audio engineers, producers, and performing artists, they must be able to take and follow directions given by many different people.

Working Conditions

Working conditions are typically comfortable, though not always. Small studios can quickly become crowded, noisy places to work, but if the audio engineer generally enjoys the music being recorded and the musicians recording it, this need not be considered a hardship. Studios are typically air-conditioned because recording equipment needs to be kept in a cool environment in order to perform at its peak. Most audio engineering is done indoors, with the exception of live performance recordings done outdoors (at concerts or festivals), so the climate is generally pleasant and controlled. Some audio engineers may also work on events, which requires them to set up equipment and check sound on the fly in various venues.

Work schedules may vary, depending on when the studio is typically open for recording. Whereas some studios operate on typical nine-to-five schedules, others cater to musicians who prefer to record late at night or into the wee hours of the morning. Audio engineers usually work forty to sixty hours a week, although this may depend on the timeline for a specific recording. Compact disc and album recordings usually take from three hundred to five hundred hours to record, but spoken-word recordings usually require only about one hundred hours.

Earning a Living

According to the Bureau of Labor Statistics (BLS), audio engineers make a median salary of $42,550 a year. The median salary for sound engineering technicians is $53,680, and audio and video equipment technicians earn about $42,230 a year. Broadcast technicians, meanwhile, receive $38,550 per year. Pay also varies depending on the industry in which one works. Those in the film and sound-recording industries typically earn a median wage of $50,230, but those in the arts, entertainment, and recreation industries earn only $42,820 a year. Audio engineers in radio and television broadcasting earn the least, with a median annual wage of $36,380. On top of that, audio engineers working in major cities tend to earn more than those in smaller cities, in keeping with higher costs of living.

What Is the Future Outlook for Audio Engineers?

The BLS predicts that employment for broadcast and sound engineering technicians will grow by 7 percent through 2024, which is considered average across all professions tracked by the government. The BLS also notes that employment for audio and visual equipment technicians will grow at a rate of 12 percent through 2024, which is faster than average. "Growth is expected to stem from businesses, schools, and radio and television stations seeking new equipment to improve their audio and video capabilities," notes the BLS's *Occupational Outlook Handbook*. "More audio and video technicians should be needed to set up new equipment or upgrade and maintain old, complex systems for a variety of organizations."[14] Indeed, businesses are increasingly using video conferencing to save employees from having to travel to attend meetings. In addition, schools at every level of education are featuring more interactive classrooms, with whiteboards and video equipment that enable teachers to offer multimedia presentations to students. Audio engineers will be needed to install, maintain, and troubleshoot this equipment and, of course, work in recording studios across the country.

Recording engineer Justin Colletti notes that despite the fact that many records are being produced independently these days, audio engineers are still in demand. "Although budgets for label projects have shrunk significantly, there are dramatically more records being made each year," he says. "While not all of them are commercial releases, and many are recorded at least in part at musician-owned home studios, these types of projects still account for a significant slice of business for many engineers. Even low-budget personal projects regularly enlist professional help in drum tracking, vocal coaching, mixing, and mastering."[15]

Find Out More

Audio Engineering Society

www.aes.org

This is a community of audio professionals that works to promote the science of audio engineering through educational opportunities, events, and online resources.

AudioNewsRoom

www.audionewsroom.net

This online music technology magazine for audio engineers features news, software and hardware reviews, and exclusive interviews with makers, developers, and artists.

Recording

www.recordingmag.com

This magazine is for the recording musician, with information relevant to aspiring and existing audio engineers, including news, reviews, resources, videos, and a beginner's series of how-to articles.

Society of Professional Audio Recording Services

www.spars.com

This network of audio production professionals offers audio recording and mastering facilities and educational opportunities for aspiring audio engineers.

Music Teacher

What Does a Music Teacher Do?

Music teachers help students learn to play instruments, read and perform music, and use their voices as instruments. There are music teachers for every instrument as well as for every style of music. Some teachers work in elementary and high schools (K–12) or in postsecondary schools, and others may serve as private tutors or instructors on a freelance basis.

Music teachers show their students various techniques related to playing an instrument. They help students learn to breathe correctly, hold their instruments properly, and position their mouths or hands correctly. They gradually give their students more-difficult pieces to perform and assign them daily exercises like scales, arpeggios, and other repetition-based drills. Many also organize recitals and concerts where their students can show off their skills to friends, family, and members of the community. Concerts and recitals teach students how to perform in public, to overcome performance-related fears like stage fright or performance anxiety, and to achieve a commanding stage presence. All of these skills are useful for students who aim to become professional musicians or strive to succeed in other public-facing positions.

Many music teachers find their job immensely satisfying. "I just like turning kids on to music," says Kathryn Smith, who teaches music and leads the Knight Vision Show Choir at Crestview High School in Convoy, Ohio. "I love music and I love working with young people. When I can just see them enjoying it and loving it and knowing that I am developing that in them to hopefully enjoy music for their life, that's probably the coolest thing about what I do."[16]

A Typical Day on the Job

Music teachers who work in a K–12 setting follow a normal school day schedule. They typically teach several music ensemble classes throughout the day and may also teach private or group lessons. Music teachers also direct bands, orchestras, and choirs, which might practice before, during, or after school. They may also run the music program for extracurricular musical activities, such as collaborative performances with the theater, dance, or art departments. Depending on their school district, music teachers usually follow a set curriculum. Private teachers have more leeway to adapt lessons to individual students' needs.

At the elementary school level, most music teachers concentrate on introducing basic concepts and teach their students how to sing together in a group. They teach students about melody and harmony, how to identify different types of instruments, and may have them play simple percussion instruments like the woodblock, cymbals, or cowbell. Older students learn more complicated instruments, such as the recorder, xylophone, or bells. However, at this age the bulk of the music curriculum will likely focus on singing, with the teacher leading the class either a cappella (without instrumental accompaniment) or using a piano or keyboard.

Kaara McHugh is an elementary music teacher in Leominster, Massachusetts. She says being able to juggle many activities and information is what makes her job interesting. "I teach general

Teaching Techniques

"Trying to use a specific method with every kid doesn't work. Neither does trying to be on an agenda about the next step. Another big mistake is not being positive. So how do you turn that around? Say things like 'Here's what to do' versus 'Don't do that.' If they're not practicing, help them understand why they should and work on something that doesn't need [practice]. Make a wild deal, joke, love them into it. Positivity is the key. Patience. Enthusiasm. Loving them into learning. Oh, and teach people you really like."

—Margie Balter, piano teacher

Quoted in CareersInMusic.com, "Become a Music Teacher." www.careersinmusic.com.

music, band, and chorus to grades K–5 which, for a classically trained soprano, is definitely a challenge," she says.

The sheer knowledge and skill sets required for these three subjects is substantial, not to mention remembering which "Johnny" is in which second grade class, what the ELA [English Language Arts] Common Core Standards are for kindergarten (important for planning lessons involving spelling and letter identification), when state testing takes place, how to upload evidence to your teaching portfolio . . . and how to handle yourself around percussionists.[17]

At the junior high school level, music teachers dive deeper into training students vocally and tend to divide them up into different types of singers: alto, soprano, baritone, and tenor, depending on how high or low they are able to sing. Music teachers at this level will often allow students to accompany songs on different instruments, such as percussion, piano, or guitar. Music teachers may choose soloists for different parts, and they will likely be in charge

A piano teacher works with her young student. Music teachers work with students to develop proper technique and an understanding of their instrument and the music they will play.

of creating a performance schedule for a school choir. Band and orchestra students may operate under the direction of a separate conductor, and all of these groups may come together to perform at school assemblies or other public events.

At the high school level, music teachers have more freedom to pursue individualized study with different groups of students. Band or orchestra directors may offer private lessons to students who play certain instruments, and they may also direct smaller groups like jazz bands, string or woodwind ensembles, chamber groups, or even piano and guitar classes. Vocal teachers typically lead the school's choir, and they may separate out different groups of singers by their vocal ranges or by the type of music they will perform (glee clubs typically perform popular music, for instance, and choirs lean more toward classical and chamber music, sometimes in foreign languages).

Music teachers at the high school level are also responsible for organizing concerts, and they may also require students to perform memorized solos at some point during the year. Part of a high school music teacher's day involves scheduling performances, choosing which pieces will be performed, rehearsing different groups, and publicizing the performances to the community.

College music professors typically teach more specialized courses on subjects like musical composition, conducting, music theory, music appreciation, music history, or pedagogy (how to teach music). They generally have more free time, given the fact that they typically teach just two or three classes per semester. As such, they may take on additional private students, or they may perform with a group to supplement their teaching income. Professors may also write, compose, or arrange music when they are not teaching.

Personality and Skills

Music teachers must possess a wide variety of skills to succeed at their job. First off, they must have musical talent. At a minimum, they should be able to play the piano and sing on key so as to demonstrate correct technique to their students. They must be able to keep good rhythm when demonstrating how to keep time. They must also be born performers, unafraid to stand up in front of a class and talk about music theory and history or belt out a tune. Indeed, music teachers are a special kind of musician—the kind that can both create music *and* inspire others to do the same.

In addition to talent, music teachers must also be very resourceful. Often faced with small (or nonexistent) budgets, they must cleverly stretch what money and resources they have at their disposal. They must also be resourceful in how they motivate their students. Everyone learns differently, and music comes more easily to some than others. It is therefore important for teachers to be able to try new ways of approaching students' problems, getting into their heads, and getting onto their level in order to help them understand musical concepts and techniques. "Great music teachers understand that every single child is capable of becoming proficient at their craft," says Grammy-nominated music teacher Anthony Mazzocchi. "Great teachers understand that

Understanding, Appreciating, and Performing Music

"11:45 a.m. Time to teach University College Understanding Music, an introduction to musical language, to a group of 15 students. I love having the opportunity to share something I am passionate about with those who are also interested and to see their understanding grow as a result. That is the best! . . . 2:00 p.m. Afternoons are spent teaching cello lessons and directing the chamber music ensembles. The ensembles perform around the [Washington] DC area, and we always want to be ready for the next performance."

—Nancy Jo Snider, music program director

Nancy Jo Snider, "Day in the Life of a Musician," College of Arts & Sciences, American University, July 17, 2014. www.american.edu.

they must help build proficient young players, one day at a time. While some students may have instant and early success, a great teacher communicates through their teaching that those who persist and practice in an intelligent and mindful way will grow, learn and reach their potential as well."[18]

Music teachers must also possess a seemingly endless supply of patience. Teaching is not always easy. Motivating students to learn new skills—particularly those that involve performing in front of others and overcoming possible embarrassment—can be tricky. But great music teachers make it seem easy. How do they do it? They are patient, kind, and endlessly helpful, offering plenty of encouragement to their students, even when they make mistakes. At the same time, music teachers should also expect their students to push themselves, even when it is difficult. As Mazzocchi explains, "The words 'that's okay' should not come out of a great teacher's mouth when students aren't holding themselves to a high standard. Great teachers are honest and tell students 'how it is,' even if it is sometimes a little blunt."[19]

Finally, music teachers must also have strong interpersonal skills. They should be able to interact with students from all walks of life, including students from different socioeconomic backgrounds, those with behavioral problems, or students who are experiencing various challenges that affect their ability to learn. They need to be open-minded about a student's perceived strengths and weaknesses. Music teachers must also be able to discuss difficult concepts in a simple way and help students articulate and achieve their musical goals.

Earning a Living

Salaries for music teachers vary according to what they teach and where they work. According to the Berklee College of Music, private instructors can make between $30 and $120 an hour, with beginning teachers charging around $45 an hour in the Boston area. Rates vary depending on a teacher's experience as well as the going rate in his or her area. Public school teachers who work in K–12 typically earn anywhere from $30,000 to about $70,000 per year. Wages vary according to the school district, as wealthier communities typically pay their teachers more. Assistant professors who work in a college or university setting typically make anywhere from $43,140 to $67,360 per year. Median wages for college professors, according to the BLS, are $75,430 per year, with music instructors earning a median wage of $68,650. For college positions, a master's degree or doctorate is typically required.

Find Out More

College Music Society
www.music.org

This is a professional society dedicated to helping university-level music teachers advance their careers. It provides the Music Vacancy List (a list of jobs in the field), mentoring, and music entrepreneurship workshops.

Music Teachers National Association

www.mtna.org

This is a valuable source of support for music teachers. The organization offers professional certification and financial assistance for continuing education in the field.

National Association for Music Education

www.nafme.org

This is a professional association for music educators that conducts research into music education issues, engages in advocacy work, and offers professional development opportunities.

National Association of Schools of Music

https://nasm.arts-accredit.org

This is an organization of schools, conservatories, colleges, and universities that establishes national standards for music degrees at the university level.

Music Therapist

What Does a Music Therapist Do?

Music therapy is a type of recreational therapy, which focuses on improving a patient's mental and physical health through some form of recreation, or play. Music therapy uses music to help patients maintain or improve their physical, social, and emotional well-being. Music therapists are responsible for assessing patients' emotional and physical states as well as their communication, social, and cognitive skills in response to music. They then design sessions that will help patients with their personal challenges. Some of the techniques music therapists use with their patients include improvisation (making music up as you go), listening to recorded music, writing songs, discussing lyrics and imagery found in different songs, or performing. Music therapists also work with doctors and specialists to create a treatment plan for each patient, so the patient's treatment is continually evaluated.

Recreational therapists typically plan and direct programs of treatment for people with illnesses, injuries, or disabilities. Music therapists use music

A music therapist works with a patient who enjoys drumming. Music therapy can help maintain or improve physical, social, and emotional well-being.

and musical performance to help their patients. Their goal is to give people a way to express themselves in a safe, friendly environment. Music helps patients tap into their subconscious and uncover feelings they may not know how to express in words. Being able to identify those feelings helps patients enrich or move forward with their lives. Music can also help relieve depression, promote self-confidence, and improve physical dexterity. Patients with problems like alcoholism and drug addiction sometimes use music therapy to overcome their substance abuse.

Patients do not need to have any particular musical talent to undergo music therapy; all they really need is an open mind and an interest in music. Music therapists work with such individuals in private or group settings or even with whole families. They also work with patients of all ages, from very young children to senior citizens.

Since the goal of music therapy is to improve a person's health, therapists often meet with a team of health care professionals to determine the best course of treatment. This helps the therapist create an appropriate program that is tailored to each patient's strengths, limitations, and personal interests. It also helps the therapist take into account what patients respond to the most, such as a particular style of music, when assessing the treatment program and its outcomes.

A Typical Day on the Job

A typical day for a music therapist varies depending on what patients the therapist is treating and where his or her work is taking place. As music therapist Kimberly Sena Moore notes on her blog, *Music Therapy Maven*, a typical session will usually have the same core components, such as an opening (perhaps singing a song of greeting or checking in with each member of the group about his or her feelings) and different types of interventions, which are ways that therapists help their clients achieve their goals.

Interventions can include playing an instrument or singing, composing songs, improvising, listening to relaxing music, analyzing lyrics, or even moving to music for physical therapy. Sessions usually end with a formal closing, such as playing a farewell song, doing a final check-in, or simply summarizing what happened during the session.

Moore notes that it is important for music therapists to consider their environment when providing therapy, as different types of lighting, outside noise, or visual distractions (like posters on a wall) can either help or hinder a client's progress. It is the therapist's job to make sure the environment is friendly, welcoming, and physically accessible. "This may seem like an odd component to add, but the environment or setting the therapist creates in the room can help or hinder the therapeutic process," says Moore. "In some ways, it's like the silent fourth player in the therapeutic process (the three key players being the therapist, the client, and the music)."[20]

Since music therapist Erin Seibert works in a psychiatric hospital, her day is a bit different from Moore's. She also describes several different stages to her day-to-day routine, including warm-ups for both voice and hands (before playing the guitar), unpacking new supplies and instruments, taking a census of hospital patients to see who has been newly admitted or discharged, assessing new patients, attending treatment team meetings, cleaning and disinfecting instruments, and documenting various patient interactions. Seibert also spends time recording all of her patients' responses to therapy, including their behavior and comments. She is also responsible for planning new therapy sessions, so she spends time brainstorming new ideas and practicing songs she wants to add to her sessions.

How Do You Become a Music Therapist?

Music therapists typically need a bachelor's degree in recreational therapy or recreation and leisure studies to begin working in the field. Recreational therapy degrees generally offer courses in human anatomy, medical and psychiatric terminology, characteristics of different illnesses and disabilities, how to use different assistive devices and technology, and patient assessment. Internships are often required as part of the degree program to give students on-the-job training.

In addition to a bachelor's degree, most hospital and other clinical employers also want employees to have certifications from the National Council for Therapeutic Recreation, such as the certified therapeutic recreation specialist credential. Therapists must also take continuing education classes to maintain their certifications, which must be renewed every five years. Some states may also require recreational therapists to become licensed by a state medical board; however, as of 2014 only New Hampshire, North Carolina, Oklahoma, and Utah required licensing.

Personality and Skills

Music therapists must possess a wide variety of skills to help their patients. Like music teachers, therapists must be kind and compassionate. They frequently deal with people who need emotional support, so they must be naturally disposed to give friendly assistance, help people express themselves, and generally be helpful.

Why Warm-Ups Matter

"A music therapist must start the day with some vocal warm-ups. No matter if voice is your main instrument, we use it a lot within music therapy. . . . This is also important for a music therapist's physical health. Recently I came down with a case of the old tendinitis because I wasn't warming up my hands/wrists/fingers before playing guitar. Physically being out of commission drastically alters our abilities to do our jobs, so it's important we have good habits for taking care of our physical-musical self."

—Erin Seibert, music therapist

Erin Seibert, "A Day in the Life of a Psychiatric Music Therapist," *Music Therapy Time* (blog). https://musictherapytime.com.

Some patients may have psychiatric or behavioral problems, so music therapists must know how to handle emotional or physical outbursts and help patients redirect their energy into something positive, such as playing a musical instrument, singing, or listening to expressive music. Compassion is at the core of a music therapist's work; the overall goal is to help patients learn to use music to positively influence their thoughts and behavior.

Music therapists must also have excellent leadership skills. They are typically responsible for planning and leading musical programs, providing interventions, and interacting with other health care providers to serve their patients. As such, music therapists must be good at both taking and giving directions. Being able to keep small and large groups on task is another skill music therapists should possess. They must make sure everyone is participating and that their programs are entertaining as well as therapeutic.

Along with leadership skills, music therapists should have active listening skills. They must pay attention to patients' problems and any issues with their treatment. Some patients may prefer more solitary music listening time, whereas others may be more interested in extroverted musical performance. Good therapists know which activities are best suited to a patient's needs. They should also be excellent communicators, able to give clear directions to their patients.

Finally, music therapists should be patient. They work with many different people, all of whom have different interests and abilities. Some patients may require additional time and attention in order to grasp certain concepts or play different instruments. Music therapists must be able and willing to devote that special attention to all participants.

Working Conditions

Music therapists typically work indoors in schools, hospitals, or nursing homes. They may also work in psychiatric facilities, rehabilitation or correctional centers, private clinics for substance abuse or pain and stress management, shelters for battered women, hospices, or day treatment centers. Working conditions can vary, depending on the employer. Music therapists typically work standard forty-hour workweeks, but they may also work extra hours in order to reach all of their patients.

A music therapist and blogger known as Roia says that one of the benefits of her profession is that there is never a dull moment. She can never truly predict what any of her patients might do, particularly since they all come from different backgrounds and have different therapeutic needs. "It's rarely dull being a music therapist," she says. "Sometimes your clients will do unexpected sorts of things, or you'll find yourself dealing with really uncomfortable feelings. [But] this is what makes this work so fascinating and so completely worthwhile!"[21]

Earning a Living

According to the Bureau of Labor Statistics (BLS), music therapists make a median wage of $45,890 per year. The Berklee College of Music points out that there can be a wide range in pay for music therapists, depending on where they work. Children's day care and preschool therapists have an average salary of $47,429. Music therapists who work in elementary and high schools earn on average $47,537, and those who work in a university setting earn about $60,340.

Therapists employed in correctional facilities receive an average salary of $49,000, and those working in nursing homes or assisted living facilities earn $42,986 per year. Self-employed music therapists in private practice can earn up to $135,000 at the high end of the pay scale, with a median yearly salary of $50,227.

What Is the Future Outlook for Music Therapists?

The BLS predicts that employment of recreational therapists, including music therapists, will grow by 12 percent through 2024, which is considered faster than average. The main reason for this predicted swell is the aging US population. Elderly people are more likely to suffer from a variety of injuries and ailments that require therapy (such as strokes and Alzheimer's disease). As a result, positions in the music therapy field will likely increase

Music, Language, and Autism

"A lot of children I work with have autism. And a common feature of autism is difficulty with language and communication. And one of the things we know is that language and singing occupy two different parts of the brain, although some of it overlaps. But it gives me a different inroad to help them learn language. And it's just amazingly exciting when I come week to week and I see progress and progress. And these kids really learn to speak using music."

—Holly Miller, music therapist

Quoted in Marketplace, "Day in the Work Life: Music Therapist." www.marketplace.org.

in places like nursing homes, adult daycare programs, and any other places that serve this population. Music therapists also frequently work in correctional facilities. The growing number of inmates in the United States may also contribute to the increased need for music therapists.

Find Out More

American Music Therapy Association
www.musictherapy.org

This organization is dedicated to aspiring and professional music therapists. It offers a variety of publications, conferences, and student organizations.

American Psychological Association
www.apa.org

The leading scientific and professional organization representing psychologists in the United States and a good source of information regarding the credentialing process a music therapist must undergo.

Imagine
www.imagine.musictherapy.biz

This annual online magazine is entirely devoted to the subject of early childhood music therapy.

World Federation for Music Therapy
www.musictherapyworld.net

This nonprofit corporation aims to promote music therapy. It puts on a conference every three years called the World Congress of Music Therapy.

Record Producer

A Few Facts

Number of Jobs

About 122,600 in 2014

Median Salary

$68,440

Educational Requirements

Bachelor's degree

Personal Qualities

Communication skills, creativity, leadership and time-management skills

Work Settings

Indoors in recording studios or private offices

Future Job Outlook

Growth of 9 percent through 2024

What Does a Record Producer Do?

Record producers work with musicians and audio engineers to create a specific sound and style for a recording. They typically aim for sounds they think will be popular with an intended audience; in rock and pop music, the goal is to create a profitable hit. They also try to create music that fits within a genre yet also makes the musicians sound unique. Producers help give an album an overall vision, which will improve its sales. According to the Berklee College of Music, a record producer helps recording artists with many details involved in recording an album, from selecting music to record, adapting arrangements, checking music licenses and copyrights, influencing mixes, working with recording engineers, and keeping tabs on the recording budget. Record producers may also help assemble a group of musicians to record the album if the artist does not already have a band.

Ideally, record producers help musicians balance decisions about recording artistry versus profits, creating songs that will both satisfy the musician's sense of artistry and encourage the public to purchase it. Many different decisions are made to create a cohesive album.

Some record producers are much more involved in the minute details of production, whereas others tend to hand off tasks to different specialists. Producers may arrange for recording studio time, technicians, and background musicians. Some are involved in mixing and editing work, creating cover art and packaging, handling contracts, or dealing with other paperwork, marketing, and promotion endeavors. Major record companies have whole departments and staff to handle such tasks, but producers who work at independent labels tend to be more hands-on. Producers at independent labels tend to also scout talent, whereas major record labels have separate artists and repertoire staff to sniff out up-and-coming bands and solo artists.

A Typical Day on the Job

Producers work with musicians and recording engineers every day. After signing a solo artist or group to their label, producers usually prepare a budget that accounts for all the expenses that will be needed to make the album. They will then book time in a recording studio, where musicians can practice and eventually lay down tracks. The producer also hires audio engineers to work on the album.

Producers ensure the recording studio is comfortable for the artists and stocked with all of the necessary instruments and equipment. When recording is under way, producers work with audio engineers to adjust sound levels, quality, and microphones and other equipment to make sure the best work is recorded. Record producer Alex Pilkington describes his production process in the following way: "I just take the raw material away and live with it for a while. Then [my partner] Mark and I deconstruct it all and start working with it."[22] Pilkington typically experiments with a variety of drumbeats to determine which genre an album will fall under, and then he begins to build the album's sound from the bottom up. Other producers choose to work from the top down,

The Decision Maker

"Essentially, all I do is help an artist record a song. What that is changes a lot. Usually it involves sitting in rehearsals, discussing the songs, suggesting changes and creating a plan for how we will record the song. In the studio, you may decide which drum kit you use, how to tune it for each song and how many microphones to put on it. You may change instruments and amplifiers for each song, and even for different parts within the one song. You can also record the vocals in many different ways. The producer makes all of these decisions."

—Australian music producer Magoo

Quoted in Bec Wolfers, "A Week in the Life of . . . a Music Producer, Magoo," Music Industry Inside Out, April 14, 2015. http://musicindustryinsideout.com.au.

starting with the vocals or lead guitar, layering on different instruments and effects as they go.

After recording, producers help the audio engineers mix and master the album. They may tell engineers to add additional instruments, vocals, or effects. The entire process can take days or weeks, depending on whether the producer is a perfectionist. Interestingly, although producers and audio engineers typically work together to create an album, today's digital techniques make it much easier for individual artists to offer their own input, and producers and engineers may find themselves left out of the equation. Pilkington says that artists' ability to mix their own music has drastically changed the modern process of record producing—something he does not think is necessarily positive. "Producers aren't producing any more, they're just tidying up," he says. "Sound engineers these days are little more than advisers to people doing their own production, which I think is sad because it's a proper trade involving a lot of knowledge. Not everyone understands microphone techniques or sound compression."[23] In any case, once the producer and artist are happy with the mix, a master (final copy) is made. Then the album is ready to be manufactured.

How Do You Become a Record Producer?

Record producers typically need to have a formal music education and a bachelor's degree in music performance or production. That said, it is even more important for producers to keep on top of changing trends and technology in the recording industry. Ultimately, there is no one path—nor even one skill set—that leads people to become great producers. Some get into the industry as musicians who help band members with production tasks, but others might be engineers or self-producers working from their own homes.

Personality and Skills

Record producers need a number of skills to be successful. Chief among these are leadership skills. Being able to take charge of any situation—especially difficult ones that feature clashing personalities and many different musicians trying to take the lead—is one of the most important things a producer can do to keep a recording schedule on track. Record producers must also act on behalf of musicians while in the recording booth, giving instructions and accepting notes. They also supervise backup musicians and technicians to make sure recording, mixing, and mastering are done right.

Record producers must also have excellent communication skills. Being a good communicator helps maintain good working relationships in a recording studio and ensures that things get done right the first time. It is also important for a producer to communicate clearly with all different kinds of people about music and technical issues.

Along with communication skills, record producers should also have terrific time-management skills. It is the producer's job to make sure a record is both on time and on budget. Therefore, producers must often nudge perfectionist musicians and engineers forward in the process. Producers need to balance their desire for perfection with their desire to finish a project. Thus, it is important for producers to keep good track of time, successfully keep musicians on task, and complete projects on time.

Working Conditions

Record producers generally work in a private office or recording studio alongside musicians and audio engineers. Producers at larger recording companies typically have a supporting staff to help them with day-to-day activities and paperwork, but those at smaller, independent labels frequently do everything themselves.

Producers often have expense accounts to travel and meet with musicians they would like to sign. This means they can often be found on the road in addition to the office or studio. Although the travel schedule may at times be demanding, music producers also work in a creative environment with musicians. They enjoy the time they get to spend in studios listening to bands and solo artists they admire.

Producing can be a stressful job due to the demand to create hits. Producers must push their musicians to achieve success, and when an album is in production, they may work for weeks without time off. Producers must also make sure musicians do not waste time in the studio because renting space is expensive and every moment counts.

Earning a Living

Record producers make anywhere from $25,000 to over $1 million a year, according to the Berklee College of Music. The Bureau of Labor Statistics (BLS) estimates that median pay for a record producer in 2015 was $68,440 per year. The world's highest-paid music producer is currently Calvin Harris, who earned $63 million in 2016. According to the website Weekend Collective, Harris "became the hottest music producer in the world thanks to a string of huge hits like 'Summer' and collaborations with superstars like Rihanna. He made history when he had eight Top 10 singles from one album, beating out even the great Michael Jackson."[24]

What Is the Future Outlook for Record Producers?

The BLS predicts that jobs for record producers will increase by 9 percent through 2024, which is considered faster than average compared to other occupations. The reason for this growth is the continuous demand for new music, which is increasingly streamed online. Since music can now be accessed 24-7, particularly via cell phones and Wi-Fi-equipped devices, consumers are demanding more new music from artists. Although production remains a very competitive field, there will ultimately be more jobs opening up as consumers continue to demand more new music.

Producers who have extensive technological skills will do best under these conditions. As the music industry continues to evolve, so do the tools required to produce albums. Although albums have become somewhat easier to produce on an average laptop, it is still necessary to have technical knowledge and years of training to turn out a professional-sounding one. Quality output ultimately requires both fine-tuned ears and many years of experience. With good business sense and technical expertise, producers can achieve success in the field.

Find Out More

National Academy of Recording Arts & Sciences

www.grammy.com

The academy presents the annual Grammy Awards for artistic achievement, technical proficiency, and overall excellence in the recording industry. Aspiring producers aim to win a Grammy, which is one of the markers of excellence for record producers in America.

Recording Industry Association of America

www.riaa.com

This is a trade organization that supports and promotes major music companies in the United States. It's a good source of information for the aspiring record producer.

Society of Professional Audio Recording Services

www.spars.com

A network of audio production professionals that offer audio recording and mastering facilities plus educational opportunities to budding record producers.

SOURCE NOTES

Musician

1. Lee Duck, "How to Book a DIY Tour Like a Pro," *Sonicbids Blog*, July 23, 2014. http://blog.sonicbids.com.
2. Quoted in Jhoni Jackson, "What a Full-Time Touring Musician's Daily Schedule Really Looks Like," *Sonicbids Blog*, May 26, 2015. http://blog.sonicbids.com.
3. Tom Hess, "How to Become a Professional Guitarist & Musician—Facts and Myths, Part 1," Tom Hess Music Corporation. https://tomhess.net.

Music Conductor and Director

4. Tara Simoncic, "I'm an Orchestra Conductor. What Do You Want to Know?," *Guardian* (Manchester, UK), July 22, 2013. www.theguardian.com.
5. Quoted in CareersInMusic.com, "Become a Conductor." www.careersinmusic.com.
6. Bureau of Labor Statistics, "Music Directors and Composers," *Occupational Outlook Handbook*, December 17, 2015. www.bls.gov.

Music Journalist

7. Lina Lecaro, "This Is My Reality as a Woman Music Journalist," *Vice*, December 30, 2015. https://noisey.vice.com.
8. Jenna Goudreau, "Top 10 Tips for Young Aspiring Journalists," *Forbes*, November 9, 2012. www.forbes.com.
9. Quoted in Dana Mathews, "Tips for the Aspiring Music Journalist, from Industry Legend Lisa Robinson," *Teen Vogue*, April 23, 2014. www.teenvogue.com.

Composer

10. Daniel Ott, "Snapshot: 'A Day in the Life of a Composer,' or 'Why I Don't Write Much Music,'" *Daniel Ott: Composer* (blog), July 4, 2012. www.danielottmusic.com.
11. Heather Fenoughty, "A Day in the Life of a Composer," *Heather Fenoughty* (blog), March 16, 2009. www.heather-fenoughty .com.

Audio Engineer

12. Recording Connection, "Life as a Recording Engineer." www .recordingconnection.com.
13. Tim O'Donovan, "A Day in the Life of an Audio Engineer," Brown Bag Films, December 4, 2013. www.brownbagfilms .com.
14. Bureau of Labor Statistics, "Broadcast and Sound Engineering Technicians," *Occupational Outlook Handbook*, December 17, 2015. www.bls.gov.
15. Justin Colletti, "Top 10 Reasons Not to Become a Recording Engineer," *Trust Me I'm a Scientist*, November 7, 2011. www .trustmeimascientist.com.

Music Teacher

16. Quoted in Ed Gebert, "A Day in the Life of . . . a Local Music Teacher," *Van Wert (OH) Times Bulletin*, January 12, 2009. http://timesbulletin.com.
17. Kaara McHugh, "Behind the Music: Life as an Elementary School Music Teacher." CollegeXpress, May 25, 2015. www .collegexpress.com.
18. Anthony Mazzocchi, "What Makes a Great Music Teacher?," National Association for Music Education, October 9, 2015. www.nafme.org.
19. Mazzocchi, "What Makes a Great Music Teacher?"

Music Therapist

20. Kimberly Sena Moore, "What Is a Typical Music Therapy Session Like?," *Music Therapy Maven* (blog), February 9, 2011. www.musictherapymaven.com.

21. *Mindful Music Therapist* (blog), "So You Want to Become a Music Therapist," November 28, 2010. https://mindfulmusic therapist.blogspot.com.

Record Producer

22. Quoted in Graham Snowdon, "A Working Life: The Music Producer," *Guardian* (Manchester, UK), May 13, 2011. www. theguardian.com.

23. Quoted in Snowdon, "A Working Life."

24. Weekend Collective, "The Highest Paid Music Producers in 2016." www.weekendcollective.com.

INTERVIEW WITH A MUSICIAN

James McGarvey is a singer/songwriter who specializes in unconventional covers of songs from the 1980s and 1990s. He discussed his career with the author via e-mail.

Q: Why did you become a musician?

A: At the age of five, I discovered that I liked being in front of a crowd with a microphone. In third grade, everyone had to participate in a hearing test before the assembly about band. We put on headphones, and they played two sounds, asking: "Is it higher, lower, or the same?" After I finished, I realized that the kids around me were struggling to tell the difference. That was the moment I discovered I had an affinity for music. I started playing the trumpet at age eight, and eventually moved on to the acoustic guitar (after my parents said no to the electric guitar), writing my own music, and performing in choirs, musical theater, and collaborating with other artists.

Q: When did you become a professional musician?

A: I was accepted to the New Hampshire All State Choir my sophomore year of high school. In our first rehearsal, the director said, "You are professionals, and you will comport yourselves as such." While she probably intended it as a tactic to keep two hundred high school kids in check, I took it to heart.

Q: Can you describe your typical workday?

A: On a gig day, the entire focus is the show: audience, space, room acoustics, requests, etc. I get to the location about an hour before I'm scheduled to begin playing, get set up, and take in the room. Even though it only takes about ten minutes from getting there to being ready to play, I don't like to be rushed before

71

a show. Typical gigs run three hours, so I'll play two forty-five-minute sets, each followed by a ten- to fifteen-minute break, then play the last hour or so straight through. If the room is hopping, I'll play a little longer. After the show, I break everything down (always wind your cords nicely, kids, trust me), and head home.

On days I don't have gigs, I'm practicing. I work on learning or perfecting covers, writing new songs, and updating older originals. I also check in with social media, record videos and songs, and look for work.

Q: What do you like most about your job?

A: I play guitar and sing in front of people; I do what I love and get paid for it. That's the dream. The rush of accomplishment from a good show makes it worthwhile. For nonperformers, the only comparison I can think of is the split second between pulling a ripcord and the parachute opening. That moment lasts forever on stage. Every song, every chord, every note could fail, and you have to trust that the years of work you've put in will be worth it: you'll hit the notes, you'll have enough breath support, and your fingers won't fail.

Q: What do you like least about your job?

A: Unresponsive rooms. The only thing more frustrating than an empty room is a room full of people who don't seem to notice you at all. I still leave it all on the stage—you never know when it's going to be your last show—but it's a hundred times harder.

Q: What personal qualities do you find most valuable for this type of work?

A: Passion. You have to love your art so much it doesn't matter how many people are listening. Fortitude. You have to be prepared for rejection. There will be people who don't like you or don't respond to you for no reason. Adaptability. No two rooms, stages, or bars will be the same. Even a space you're familiar with can change from show to show.

Q: What advice do you have for students who might be interested in this career?

A: Write the bad song. Not all of your songs will be good, but if you don't get them out of your head, you won't be able to get past it. Research all the ways you can be involved in music. Producing, writing, performing. Discover new music. Even if you think you don't like a genre, give it a chance. Figure out *why* you like or dislike a song. Study the greats, study the one-hit wonders, study. Learn how to present yourself onstage.

If this is what you want to do, you have to be prepared to make your dreams happen. Most artists aren't lucky enough to be discovered at a gas station or on the Internet—they have to go searching for any and all opportunities to perform. To quote [musician and producer] Quincy Jones: "You gotta do what you love and really believe in it, because that is your truth."

OTHER CAREERS IF YOU LIKE MUSIC

Accompanist
Archetier (bow maker for
    stringed instruments)
Artists and repertoire
    coordinator
Background singer
Booking agent
Business manager
Busker
DJ
Drum major
Entertainment attorney
Festival director
Field merchandiser
Instrument builder
Jingle writer
Licensing representative
Lighting technician
Luthier (maker of stringed
    instruments)
Marketing coordinator
Music photographer

Music promoter
Nightclub manager
Opera singer
Orchestra member
Personal manager
Pipemaker
Piano tuner
Podcaster
Program director
Promotion manager
Publicist
Publisher
Roadie
Session musician
Sound technician
Stage manager
Talent booker
Talent scout
Tour bus driver
Tour manager
Vocalist

Editor's note: The online *Occupational Outlook Handbook* of the US Department of Labor's Bureau of Labor Statistics is an excellent source of information on jobs in hundreds of career fields, including many of those listed here. The *Occupational Outlook Handbook* may be accessed online at www.bls.gov/ooh.

INDEX

77

PICTURE CREDITS

ABOUT THE AUTHOR

Laura Roberts writes fiction and nonfiction for young adults and adults. She has worked as a weekly columnist, writing coach, professional book reviewer, and editor. She lives in San Diego, California, with her husband, Brit.